WRITER'S HANDBOOK

PATHWAYS
Journey to Excellence through Literacy

KENDALL/HUNT PUBLISHING COMPANY
4050 Westmark Drive   Dubuque, Iowa 52002

AUTHOR TEAM

Terry Heinecke   Jean Sherlock
Kim O'Brien   Sandra McEowen
Joyce Bieber   Pam Vincent

PATHWAYS EDITION

Charlene Lavallee
Frances Schander
Sharon Searson

Copyright © 2007, by Kendall/Hunt Publishing Company

ISBN: 978-0-7575-2751-7

All rights reserved. No part of this publication may be reproduced, stored in a retrieval system, or transmitted, in any form or by any means, electronic, mechanical, photocopying, recording, or otherwise, without the prior written permission of the copyright owner.

Printed in the United States of America

THE WRITER'S HANDBOOK
Grade One
Table of Contents

1. ABC ORDER 1

2. SENTENCES .3
   Kinds of Sentences 3
   Noun 4
   Verb 4

3. CAPITAL LETTERS 5

4. PUNCTUATION MARKS 7
   Period 7
   Question Mark 7
   Exclamation Mark 7
   Comma .8

5. PROCESS WRITING—HOW TO
   BEGIN WRITING 9
   Prewriting 9
   Prewriting/Drafting 12
   Revising 12
   Editing/Proofreading 14

6. WRITING 15
Forms of Writing 15
- Friendly Letter 15
- Envelope 16
- Narrative Writing 17

Kinds of Writing 18
- Fairy Tales 18
- Fantasy 18
- Fiction 18
- Folklore 19
- Folktales 19
- Nonfiction/Factual 19
- Parables 19
- Poetry 20

Parts of a Book 20
- Title Page 20
- Copyright Date 21
- Dedication Page 21
- Table of Contents 22
- About the Author
  and Illustrator 22

7. COMMONLY USED WORDS 23

8. WORD LISTS 43
   Color Words 43
   Animal Names 44
   Animal Moms and Babies 44
   Holidays and Special Days 45
   Number Words 46
   Question Words 51
   Words to Know About:
     Antonyms, Synonyms,
     Homophones 51
   Days of the Week,
     Months of the Year 53
   Other Abbreviations 55
   Contractions 55

INDEX 59

ABC Order

The order of letters from A to Z is called ABC order (alphabetical order). ABC order always stays the same. Listed below are the letters of the alphabet in ABC order.

a b c d e f g h i j k l m n o p q r s t u v w x y z
A B C D E F G H I J K L M N O P Q R S T U V W X Y Z

Words can be put into ABC order. Use the first letter of each word to put it in ABC order. Listed below are some words in ABC order.

ant	fin	let	rat
bug	goat	man	sun
cat	happy	net	tree

Sometimes the first letter in two words are the same. Then the second letter of each word needs to be used to put the word in ABC order.

These words are in ABC order:

c<u>a</u>t	m<u>i</u>tt	t<u>a</u>nk
c<u>u</u>b	m<u>o</u>on	t<u>e</u>nt
m<u>a</u>t	m<u>u</u>d	t<u>r</u>ain

Sentences

A sentence tells a complete thought. It always begins with a capital letter and ends with a punctuation mark. Every sentence contains a noun and a verb.

The tiger roared.

Do you want olives on your pizza?

Kinds of Sentences

There are four kinds of sentences.

A statement is a sentence that tells a complete thought. It always begins with a capital letter and ends with a period (.).

Juan and Pedro played ice hockey.

A question is a sentence that asks something. It always begins with a capital letter and ends with a question mark (?).

Are Juan and Pedro playing now?

An exclamation is a sentence that shows strong feeling. It always begins with a capital letter and ends with an exclamation mark (!).

We won!

An imperative is a sentence that shows strong feelings. It often gives a command. It always begins with a capital letter and ends in an exclamation mark (!).

Go to your room!

Noun

A noun is a word that names a person, place, or thing.

person—boy, girl, mom, dad

place—school, home, store

thing—table, chair, paper, cake

Verb

A verb is a word that most often shows an action.

jump, sit, walk, run

Capital Letters

The beginning letter in important words is written with a capital letter.

Name of people, places   **Holidays**
First word in a sentence   **Cities**
Months of the year   **States, Provinces, Countries**
Days of the week   **Book titles**

Some words always begin with a capital letter.

I   Holy Spirit
Jesus   Seventh-day Adventist
God   North America
Christ   United States
Bible   Canada
Sabbath

Punctuation Marks

Punctuation marks are used in a sentence to make it clearer and easier to understand. These marks tell the reader when to stop, pause, ask a question, show excitement, or separate words.

Period

A period (.) is used at the end of a sentence that tells something.

The balloon is blue.

Question Mark

A question mark (?) is used at the end of a sentence that asks something.

Will you please bring me the book?

Exclamation Mark

An exclamation mark (!) is used at the end of a sentence that shows excitement.

Watch Out!

Comma

A comma (,) is used for a pause in a sentence or to separate a list of words.

Please bring me the ball, and then we'll have fun.

Please bring cake, ice cream, and candles.

Process Writing— How to Begin Writing

Prewriting—Finding Ideas to Write About

Write down all the ideas you can think of. Choose one idea to write about.

Here is one example of writing about pets:

Brainstorming

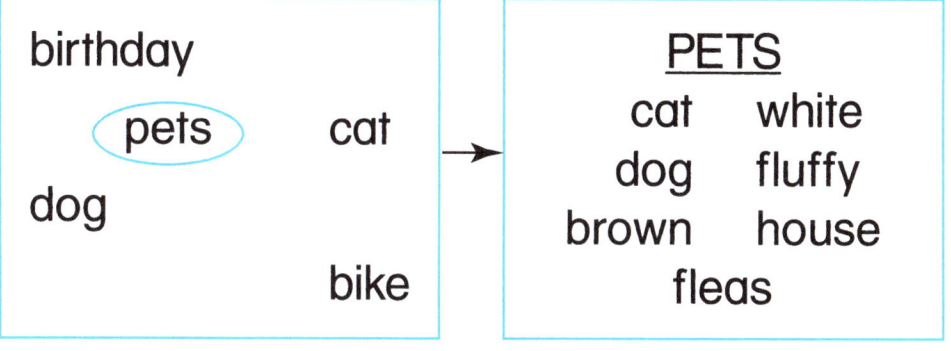

A web or map can help bring out parts of a story.

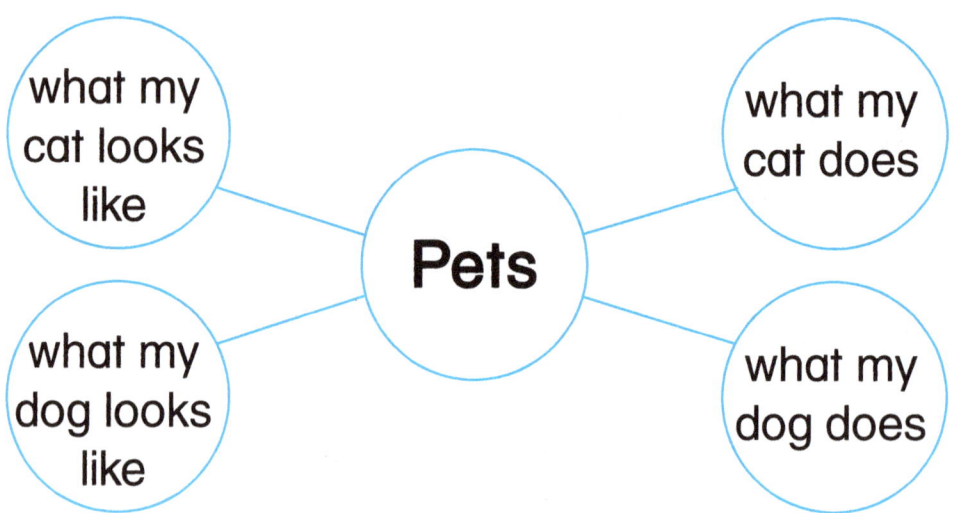

Think of the parts of a story you could write. Find an idea to write about in daily writing journals.

Draw or write about the beginning, the middle, and the end.

MY BALLOON

Kim gave me a balloon.	I liked my balloon.	I played with my balloon.
Then I fell down.	My balloon went up. It was lost.	Kim gave me a new balloon.

Read books for writing ideas.

Prewriting/Drafting

Use your prewriting activities to give you an idea for writing a story.

- Write down all your ideas and choose one.
- Draw your story ideas and write about one.
- Make a web to think of story parts.
- Choose an idea from your journal to write about.

Revising

1. As you read your story, ask yourself these questions:
   - Is there a beginning, middle, and end?
   - Do all of the words make sense?
   - What can I do to make it better?
   - Ask a friend to listen to your story. Does your friend have any helpful ideas to make your story better?

2. Look for mistakes.

   Mark the mistakes with Editor's Marks.

Symbol	Meaning
◯	Check spelling.
ℒ	Delete or remove.
∧	Add a letter, word, sentence, etc.
⊙	Add a period.
ˆ,	Add a comma.
ˇ'	Add an apostrophe.
≡	Make a capital letter.
/	Make the letter lowercase.

Fix the mistakes for your final draft.

Editing/Proofreading

Use this writer's checklist when you proofread your story.

- Make any changes in your story. Recopy it using your best handwriting.
- Did I put my name on my paper?
- Did I use capital letters where needed?
- Did I put in all the punctuation marks?
- Did I check my spelling?

Writing

Forms of Writing

Friendly Letter

A friendly letter is written to a friend. This letter tells about interesting events and asks questions about the friend. The friendly letter has five parts: the heading, greeting, body, closing, and signature.

Example:

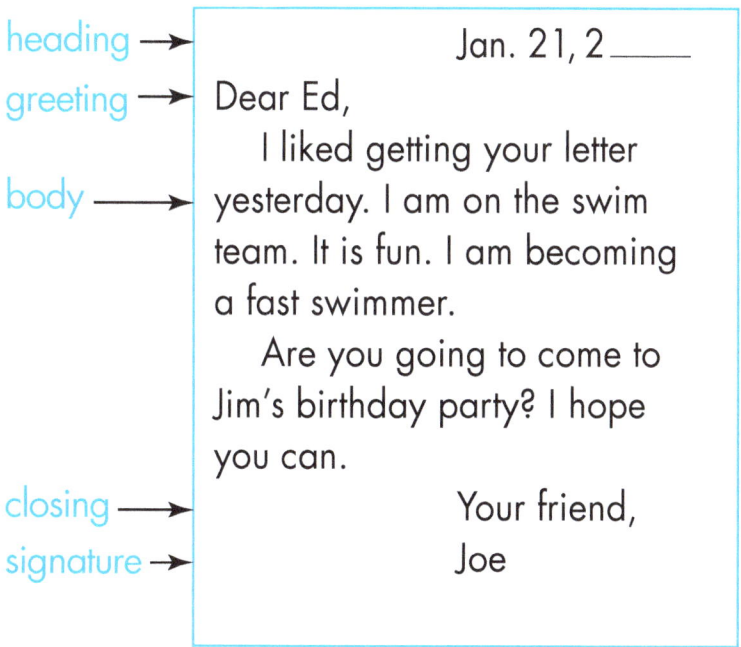

Envelope

A letter is put inside an envelope and then mailed. An envelope has three parts. Each part must be in a certain place on the envelope.

1. The mailing address tells who the letter will be mailed to.
2. The return address tells who is sending the letter.
3. The stamp pays the post office to deliver the letter.

Envelopes going to other countries must always have the country's name.

Narrative Writing

Narrative writing tells a story. It has a beginning, middle, and end.

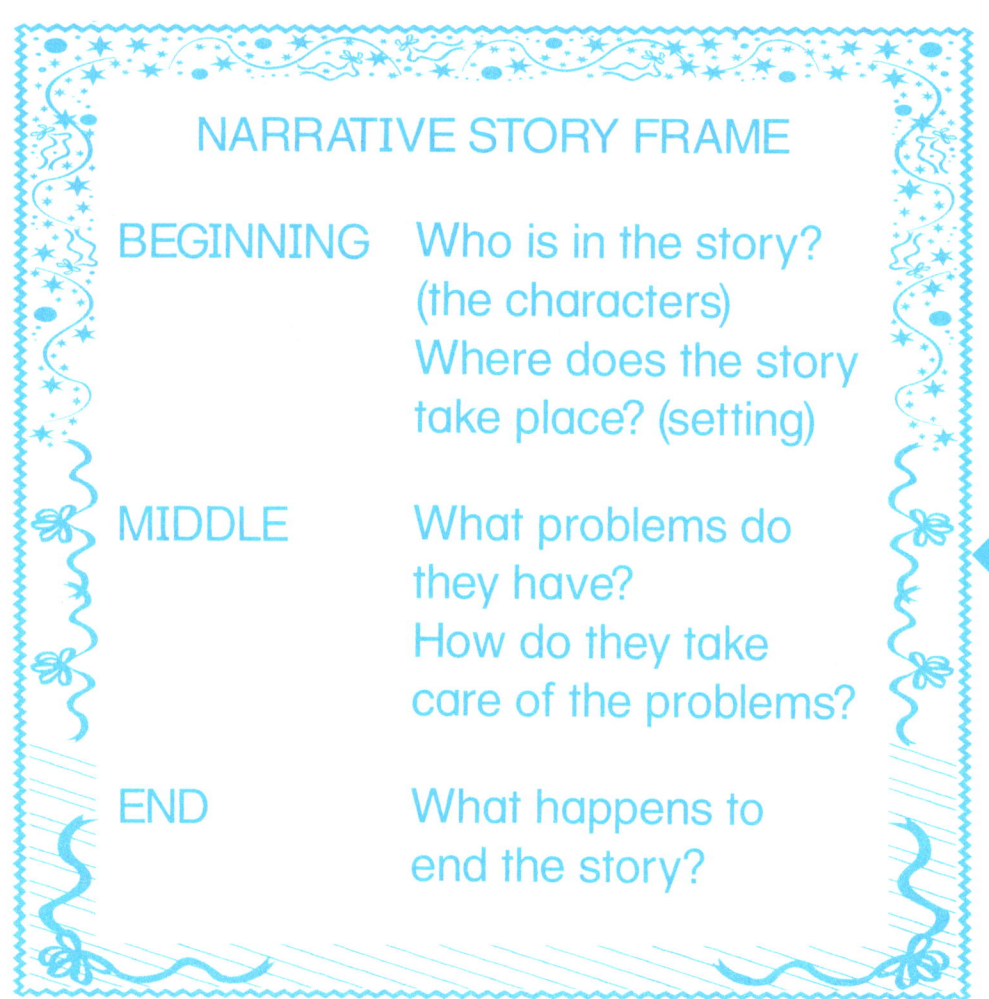

NARRATIVE STORY FRAME

BEGINNING   Who is in the story? (the characters)
Where does the story take place? (setting)

MIDDLE   What problems do they have?
How do they take care of the problems?

END   What happens to end the story?

Kinds of Writing

There are many different kinds of writing. Here are some kinds:

Fairy Tales

Fairy tales are old made-up stories that have good or evil characters. Magic is often included in a fairy tale, and these tales are often about princesses, princes, and kings. They often end with ". . . and they lived happily ever after."

Fantasy

A fantasy is a story that cannot really happen. In this type of story, people or animals may pretend to do something that cannot really happen.

Fiction

Fiction stories tell about people, places, and things that seem real but are not. They are made up by an author.

Folklore

Folklore are stories that were retold long before the words were ever written down. These stories may begin with "Once upon a time" or "Long, long, ago." They may or may not be true stories.

Folktales

Folktales are stories that were made up long ago. These stories tell how something came to be or teach a lesson. After listening to folktales while growing up, these grown-ups would tell their children the same tales. Animals in folktales often think and talk like people. People in folktales are often silly.

Nonfiction/Factual

Nonfiction stories are true stories about people, places, and things.

Parables

Parables are made-up or real stories that tell a moral or religious lesson. Jesus told parables to teach us lessons.

Poetry

Poems are sets of words that are song-like. Poems can rhyme, tell a story, or create a feeling. Writing poems is like painting a picture with words. Poems are often said or read aloud. Here is a poem for you to read:

Color
Red is a sweet smelling rose.
Orange is the bright shining sky.
Green is the corn growing tall.
Black is the day when it is done.

Parts of a Book

Publishing is a way to share your writing. Some examples of publishing are author's corner, school paper, letters and books. A published book has these parts:

Title Page

The title page tells three things:
1. The book title
2. The author—the person who wrote the book
3. The illustrator—the person who drew the pictures

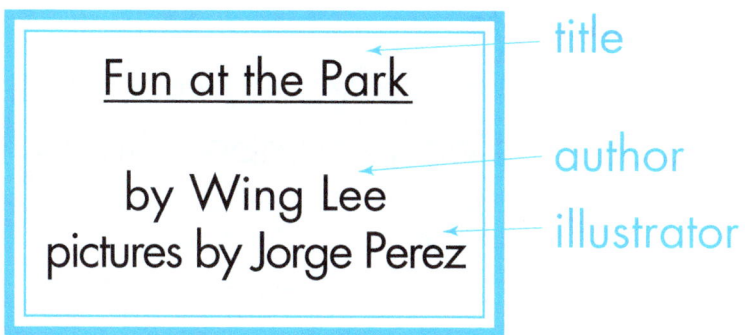

Copyright Date

The copyright date is the year the book is published. It goes on the back of the title page and has a symbol:

Copyright © 2007 by Kendall/Hunt Publishing Co.

Dedication Page

If the book is written for someone special, the author writes that person's name on the dedication page.

Dedicated to my friend Raoul.

Table of Contents

The table of contents tells the names of the chapters and the page numbers where the chapters begin.

Contents
The Kite.................................3
The Hike..............................11
A Good Game....................16

About the Author and Illustrator

This part tells the reader about the author's real life. It can tell about the illustrator, too.

About the Author
Wing lives in New York.
He is now in first grade.
Wing likes to draw and . . .

Commonly Used Words

The following words are some of the most commonly used words in writing. They are written in ABC order.

Aa

a
add
Adventist
after
age
ago
air
all
also
and

angel
any
apple
are
as
ask
at
author
away

Bb

baby

bad

banana

be

bed

been

belong

Bermuda

Bible

big

boat

books

box

bread

bright

bring

but

by

Cc

cake

came

Canada

candy

card

Christian

church

class

clean

close

coat

color

come

cook

copyright

could

cousin

cover

cow

cut

Dd

dad

dance

date

day

dear

deer

depart

did

dime

dish

do

dogs

doll

dollar

done

door

down

Ee

each
early
earth
east
eat
edge

edit
end
enough
even
every

Ff

face
fall
family
fast
feet
fill
find
fire

first
fish
flower
food
for
from
funny

Gg

game

gas

gave

get

glad

go

goal

God

good

got

grade

grandma

grandpa

graph

grass

grow

gum

Hh

had
hair
half
hand
happy
hard
has
have
he

heaven
help
her
here
hill
him
his
home
house

Ii

I
ice cream
if
illustrate
in

into
is
island
it

Jj

jam
Jesus
jet
job
jog
joke
jolly

joy
jug
jump
jungle
junk
just

Kk

kangaroo
keep
key
kid
kill
kind

king
kiss
kitchen
kitten
know

Ll

lake
land
last
left
like
lion
list
little

long
look
lost
love
low
luck
lunch

Mm

mad

made

make

man

may

maybe

me

milk

mine

mom

money

monkey

moon

more

most

much

my

myself

Nn

name	night
napkin	no
near	noise
neck	noon
need	north
new	not
next	note
nice	now
nickel	

Oo

of
off
okay
old
on
one
only

open
order
our
out
outline
outside
over

Pp

page
parable
park
part
pay
penny
people
pet
pie

pig
pipe
place
plant
play
please
pray
promise
put

Qq

quart
quarter
queen
question

quiet
quit
quite

Rr

rabbit
race
rain
ran
read
rest
rich
ride

right
ring
river
robot
rocket
room
rose
run

Ss

Sabbath
sad
same
sat
save
saw
school
second
see
seem

send
sing
sleep
small
snow
some
south
stay
sun

Tt

take
talk
teacher
tell
thank
the
their
there
they're
thing

think
third
time
today
tomorrow
tonight
took
train
tree
trip

Uu

uncle
under
unit
United States
unless

up
upon
us
use

Vv

valentine
van
vase
vegetable
verse
very
village

vine
violet
violin
virus
visit
voice

Ww

walk

wall

was

water

week

well

went

were

west

what

when

will

wind

window

with

wood

word

work

worship

Xx

x-ray

Yy

yard yet
year you
yell young
yes your
yesterday

Zz

zero zoo
zipper

Word Lists

Color Words

Color words to write about.

red

yellow

blue

green

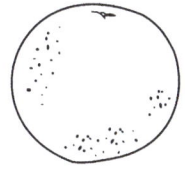
orange

purple

pink

gray

brown

white

black

Animal Names

bear	lion
cat	monkey
dog	pony
dinosaur	rabbit
elephant	whale
giraffe	zebra
horse	

Animal Moms and Babies

cat	→	kitten
cow	→	calf
dog	→	puppy
fox	→	kit
hen	→	chick
horse	→	foal
pig	→	piglet
sheep	→	lamb

Holidays and Special Days

Capital letters are used at the beginning of each word.

 New Year's Day

 Thanksgiving

 Valentine's Day

 St. Patrick's Day

 Mother's Day

 Father's Day

 Christmas

Number Words

A number can be written as a numeral or as a word.

0	→	zero	10	→	ten
1	→	one	11	→	eleven
2	→	two	12	→	twelve
3	→	three	13	→	thirteen
4	→	four	14	→	fourteen
5	→	five	15	→	fifteen
6	→	six	16	→	sixteen
7	→	seven	17	→	seventeen
8	→	eight	18	→	eighteen
9	→	nine	19	→	nineteen

More Numbers

20 twenty

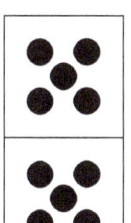 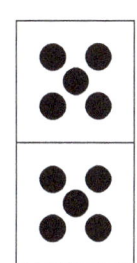

30 thirty

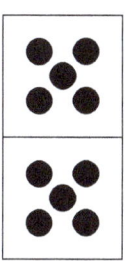  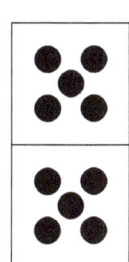

40 forty

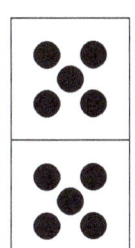 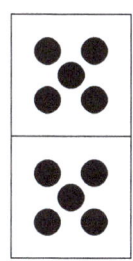 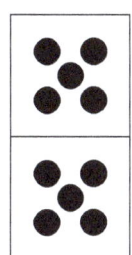 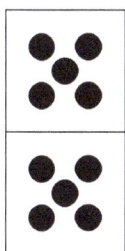

50 fifty

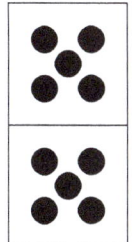 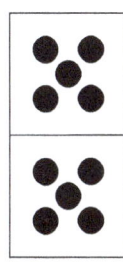 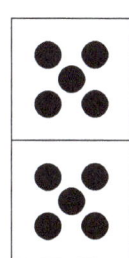 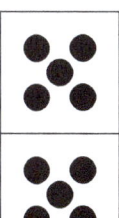 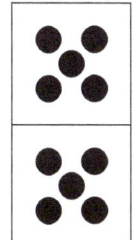

60 sixty

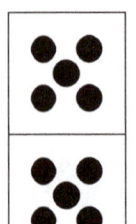 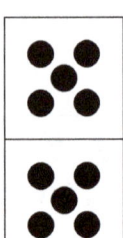 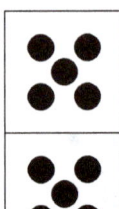 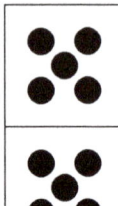 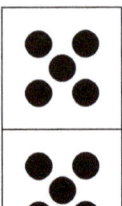 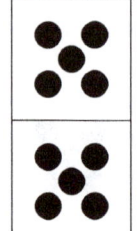

70 seventy

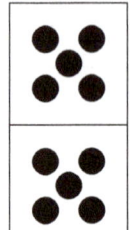 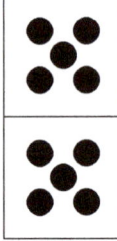 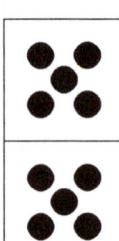 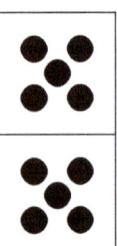

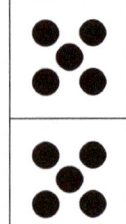 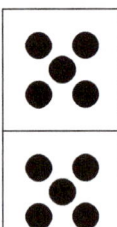 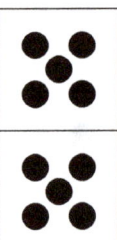

80 eighty

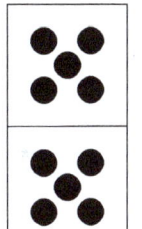 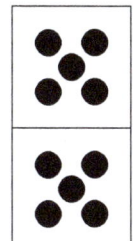 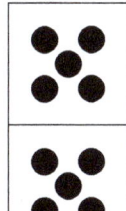 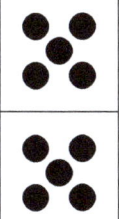

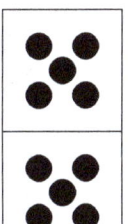 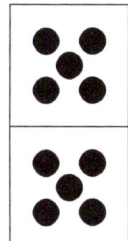 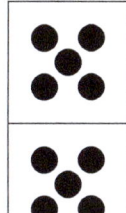 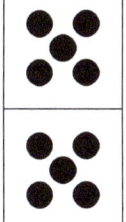

90 ninety

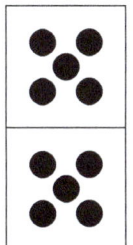 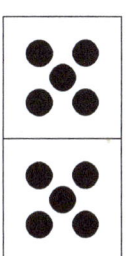 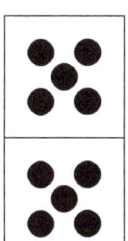 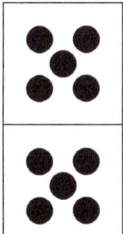 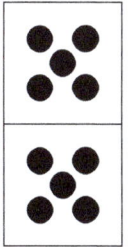

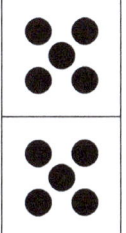 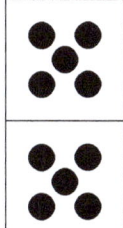 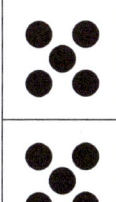 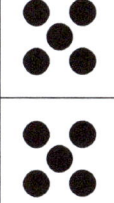

100 one hundred

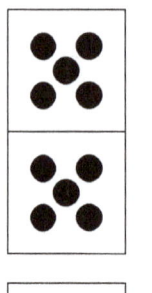 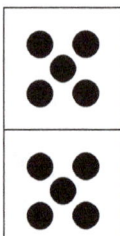 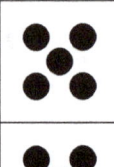 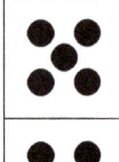 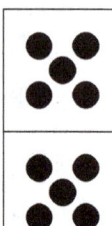

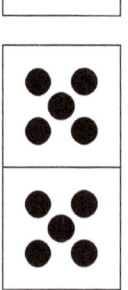 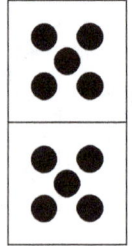 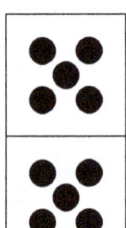 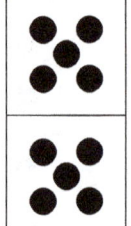 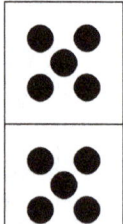

Question Words

Question words are used to start sentences that ask questions.

1. Do
2. Can
3. What
4. Are
5. Will
6. Is
7. Did
8. Has
9. Who
10. Where
11. Why
12. How
13. Does
14. When

Words to Know About: Antonyms, Synonyms, Homophones

Antonyms are words that have opposite meanings.

cold	→	hot	good	→	bad
in	→	out	go	→	stop
big	→	little	early	→	late
up	→	down	new	→	old
boy	→	girl	day	→	night

Synonyms are words that have almost the same meanings.

angry	→	mad	house	→	home
big	→	huge	neat	→	tidy
call	→	shout	sad	→	unhappy
fix	→	repair	talk	→	speak

Homophones are words that sound the same but have different spellings.

ate	→	eight	meat	→	meet
be	→	bee	sea	→	see
flew	→	flu	son	→	sun
know	→	no	weak	→	week

Days of the Week, Months of the Year

Days of the week and months of the year can be written as a whole word or as a shortened word called an abbreviation. Most abbreviations end with a period.

Days and their Abbreviations

Sunday	→	Sun.
Monday	→	Mon.
Tuesday	→	Tues.
Wednesday	→	Wed.
Thursday	→	Thurs.
Friday	→	Fri.
Saturday	→	Sat.

Months and their Abbreviations

(Short months do not have abbreviations)

January → Jan.

February → Feb.

March → Mar.

April → Apr.

May → May

June → June

July → July

August → Aug.

September → Sept.

October → Oct.

November → Nov.

December → Dec.

Other Abbreviations

Some words also have abbreviations. These letters are always followed by a period.

etc.	→	and so on	Mrs.	→	misses
Dr.	→	doctor	mo.	→	month
Mr.	→	mister	yr.	→	year

Contractions

A contraction is a short way of writing two words together. Some letters are left out in a contraction. An apostrophe (') takes the place of missing letters.

are contractions

you are	→	you're
we are	→	we're
they are	→	they're
I am	→	I'm

not contractions

is not → isn't

has not → hasn't

will not → won't

can not → can't

did not → didn't

do not → don't

is contractions

she is → she's

he is → he's

it is → it's

that is → that's

what is → what's

will contractions

I will → I'll

you will → you'll

we will → we'll

they will → they'll

she will → she'll

he will → he'll

Index

Abbreviations
   of day words, 53
   of month words, 54
   other, 55
ABC order, 1
   in commonly used words, 23–41
Alphabetical order. See ABC order
Animals
   in fantasy story, 18
   in folktales, 19
   names of, 44
      moms and babies, 44
Antonyms, 51
Apostrophe, 55
Are contractions, 55
Author
   about the, 22
   of fiction, 18
   on title page, 20
A words, 23

Body (of friendly letter), 15
Book
   parts of, 20–22
   title of, 5, 20
B words, 24

Capital letters
   first word in sentence, 3–4
   holidays, 45
   important words, 5
   special days, 45
Closing of friendly letter, 15
Color words, 43
Comma (,), 8
Commonly used words, 23–41
Contractions, 55
   are, 55
   is, 56
   not, 56
   will, 57

Copyright date, 21
C words, 25

Days, 53
   abbreviations of, 53
   capital letter in, 5
Dedication page, 21
Drafting, 12
D words, 26

Editor's marks, 13
Envelope, 16
Exclamation, 7
Exclamation mark (!), 7
E words, 27

Factual stories. See Nonfiction
Fairy tales, 18
Fantasy, 18
Fiction, 18
Final draft, 13
Folklore, 19
Folktales, 19
Friendly letter, 15
F words, 27

Greeting in friendly letter, 15
G words, 28

Heading in friendly letter, 15
Holidays, 45
   capital letter in, 45
Homophones, 52
H words, 29

Ideas, story, 9–12
Illustrator
   about the, 22
   on title page, 20
Imperative, 4
Is contractions, 56
I words, 30

Journal
   ideas for writing in, 10
J words, 30

K words, 31

Letter
   envelope for, 16
   friendly, 15
Letters
   lowercase (a–z), 1
   capital, 5, 45
   uppercase (A–Z), 1
L words, 31

Magic
   in fairytales, 18
Mailing address, 16
Mistakes in writing
   marking with editor's marks, 13
Months
   abbreviations of, 54
   capital letter in, 5
   of year, 54
M words, 32

Names, capitalizing, 5
Narrative writing, 17
Nonfiction, 19
Not contractions, 56
Noun, 4
Number words, 46–49
Numeral, 46
N words, 33

O words, 34

Parables, 19
People. *See also* Person
   in fantasy story, 18
   in fiction story, 18
   in folktales, 19
   names capitalized, 5
   true stories about, 19
Period (.)
   after abbreviations, 55
   at sentence end, 7

Person. *See also* People
   as noun, 4
Place
   as noun, 4
   important place names
      capitalized, 5
   in fiction, 18
   true stories about, 19
Poem, 20
Prewriting, 9
Process writing
   editing, 14
   final draft, 14
   first draft, 12
   prewriting (brainstorming), 9–10
   proofreading, 14
   publishing, 20
   revising, 12–13
Proofreading, 14
Publishing, 20
Punctuation marks, 7
   apostrophe ('), 55
   comma (,), 8
   exclamation mark (!), 7
   period (.), 7
   question mark (?), 7
P words 35

Question, 3
Question mark (?), 3
Question words, 51
Q words, 36

Return address, 16
Revising, 12–13
R words, 36

Sentences
   capitalize first word in, 3, 5
   kinds of, 3–4
   pause in, 8
   punctuation marks in, 3, 7–8
Signature, 15
Stamp, 16
States
   capitalized, 5

Statement, 3
Stories
   fairy tales, 18
   fantasy, 18
   fiction, 18
   folklore, 19
   folktales, 19
   ideas for, 9–12
   narrative, 17
      parts of, 17
   nonfiction, 19
   web or map for, 10
Synonyms, 52
S words, 37

Table of contents, 22
Thing
   in fiction story, 18
   as noun, 4
   in nonfiction, 19
Title page, 20
T words, 38

U words, 39

Verb, 3, 4
V words, 39

Week, 53
   days of capitalized, 5
Will contractions, 57
Word lists
   animal names, 44
      moms and babies, 44

abbreviations
   days of week, 53
   months of year, 54
   other, 55
antonyms, 51
color words, 43
contractions, 55–57
days of the week, 53
holidays, 45
homophones, 51
months of the year, 54
number words, 46–50
question words, 51
synonyms, 51
Writer's checklist, 14
Writing. *See also Process Writing*
   forms of, 15–17
   kinds of, 18–20
   narrative, 17
W words, 40

X words, 41

Year
   months of, 54
Y words, 41

Z words, 41

CPSIA information can be obtained
at www.ICGtesting.com
Printed in the USA
BVHW010026290720
584899BV00002B/4